TAKE ACTION WITH ANIMALS!

ANIMALS IN THE SKY

Written by
Madeline Tyler

Illustrated by
Amy Li

WINDMILL BOOKS

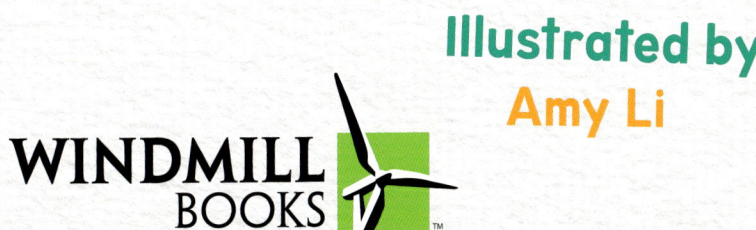

Published in 2022 by Windmill Books,
an Imprint of Rosen Publishing
29 East 21st Street, New York, NY 10010

© 2020 Booklife Publishing
This edition is published by arrangement with Booklife Publishing

All rights reserved. No part of this book may be reproduced in any form without permission in writing from the publisher, except by a reviewer.

Edited by: John Wood
Illustrated by: Amy Li

Cataloging-in-Publication Data

Names: Tyler, Madeline. | Li, Amy.
Title: Animals in the sky / by Madeline Tyler, illustrated by Amy Li.
Description: New York : Windmill Books, 2022. | Series: Take action with animals!
Identifiers: ISBN 9781499487381 (pbk.) | ISBN 9781499487404 (library bound) | ISBN 9781499487398 (6 pack) | ISBN 9781499487411 (ebook)
Subjects: LCSH: Birds--Juvenile fiction. | Bats--Juvenile fiction. | Sugar glider--Juvenile fiction. | Butterflies--Juvenile fiction.
Classification: LCC PZ7.1.T954 An 2022 | DDC [E]--dc23

Printed in the United States of America

CPSIA Compliance Information: Batch CSWM22: For Further Information contact Rosen Publishing, New York, New York at 1-800-237-9932

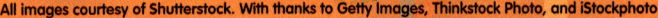

All images courtesy of Shutterstock. With thanks to Getty Images, Thinkstock Photo, and iStockphoto.

Cover – KateChe, YamabikaY, Toluk, flovie, Ellika, masher, Ann.and.Pen, exile_artist, Fears. Recurring backgrounds – YamabikaY. Recurring texture brushes – Toluk (grunge), flovie (spotty), Anna Timoshenko (rock cracks). 4–7 –Dolka, Incomible, EV-DA, 8–11 –Iveta Angelova, mexico70, nubenamo, Katerina Pereverzeva, 12–15 –PinkPueblo, nubenamo, Ursa Major, Karbo_Kreto, 16–19 – Amma Shams, ekler, Fears, Karbo_Kreto, Ms Moloko, nubenamo, Natykach Nataliia, Ursa Major, 20–23 –Anna Timoshenko, masher, PixieMe.

Can you use your imagination to take a trip into the sky?

Follow the **INSTRUCTIONS** on each page and see what you can find.

There is a **butterfly** hiding in the leaves.

STROKE

its body and then turn the page...

Now its wings are open!

SHAKE

the book and turn the page.

What do you think will happen?

Wow! Those feathers are very colorful!

Can you see the **sugar glider** in the tree?

BLOW

on the page to help it glide.

What bird is sitting up there?

Can you **TAP** its head to make it turn around?

It is an
owl!

It is time for this **bat** to go to bed.

Spin this book

UPSIDE DOWN

and turn the page...

Shh!

The bat has gone to sleep.

What colors can you see?

24